I0839592

NEW YORK TIMES BESTSELLER
TRUMP WORLD
DONALD TRUMP MUST BE STOPPED!!!
#1
CONSPIRACY BOOKS
PRESIDENT DONALD TRUMP IS DESTROYING THE UNITED STATES.FIND OUT ALL ABOUT THE SCANDALOUS SECRETS HE HAS HIDDEN.CONSPIRACY BOOK

What is Donald Trump's role in the Illuminati? Conspiracy theories on new US President.

For Believers In The Illuminati Conspiracy President of The United States Has Been Automatically Labelled A Key Member Of The Alleged Secret Society.

Did You know That There Is No such thing as Democracy In The United States Are Majority Of The World.

Let's Look up The Word Democracy For a minute.

<u>**De·moc·ra·cy**</u>

1. a system of government by the whole population or all the eligible members of a state, typically through elected representatives.
   "capitalism and democracy are ascendant in the third world"

   - a state governed by a democracy.
     plural noun: **democracies**

     "a multiparty democracy"

   - control of an organization or group by the majority of its members.
     "the intended extension of industrial democracy.

Most Americans believe that when they vote their votes count and they truly think That They Are deciding which President is being chosen but in truth the President Was Picked years ago and They're only, Observing and judging Humans State of minds.

There is only one thing your votes are used for," and that's OBSERVATION AND CONTROL!!!

Let's me Start Off By Proving with evidence that the President's are handpicked years before by the Satanic Rulers Of The World they are only puppet's the Synagogue Of Satan!

Ephesians 6:12-13 Quotes Clearly that:

"For we wrestle not against flesh and blood, but against principalities, against powers, against the rulers of the darkness of this world."

SATANIC RULERS
READ THIS
BEFORE
JOINING THE
FREEMASONS!!!
FACT: 90% OF THE WORLD
IS RAN BY
FAKE JEWS, FREE MASONS
AND THEIR GOD LUCIFER!!!
By. ANTONIO EMMANUEL

President Obama, President Trump, President Clinton , Bill Gates, Saddam Hussein, Hitler and many others are Predicted with pictures 15 years before they came into power to become Presidents And Powerful Leaders of the World In The Illuminati Card Game. Now people if you are like me there is no way in hell that this is a coincidence *Wake Up Everyone!*

The card (above) is said to show the face Donald Trump pulls in the 2011 image.

The Princess Di card from the same Illuminati game.

Illuminati card game that 'foretold 9/11 and Diana's death' predicts 'Trump assassination'

US PRESIDENT DONALD TRUMP COULD BE ASSASSINATED BY THE ALLEGED ILLUMINATI SECRET SOCIETY if a "prediction" in a 20 year-old card game is to be believed.

Illuminati: The Game of Conspiracy was released in 1995, and is said to have predicted 9/11 and Princess Diana's death.

Now, conspiracy theorists, who believe the game's creator Steve Jackson foretold world events with the cards, claim one of them warns of Mr Trump's assassination at the hands of the Illuminati.

The Illuminati conspiracy theory revolves around an alleged secret society that actually runs all global governments from behind the scenes and is slowly implementing a so-called New World order (NWO), that will culminate in a global leadership.

The theory varies in extremities, including the Illuminati being a highly Satanic cult that intends returning the devil to Earth.

<u>Conspiracy theorists</u> disagree on Mr. Trump's alleged role with the Illuminati.

Illuminati is a Conspiracy Card Game made by Steve Jackson Games (SJG),

Inspired by the 1975 book, The Illuminatus! Set of three, by Robert Anton Wilson and Robert Shea.

The amusement has foreboding mystery social orders rivaling each other to control the world through different means, including legitimate, illicit, and even magical. It was planned as an "offhanded as opposed to serious" go up against paranoid fears. It contains bunches named correspondingly to certifiable associations, for example, the Society for Creative Anachronism and the

Symbionese Liberation Army.

It can be played by two to eight players. Contingent upon the quantity of players, a diversion can take in the vicinity of one and six hours.

In September 1981, Steve Jackson and his general independent cover craftsman Dave Martin talked about their mutual profound respect of the Illuminatus! Set of three, and the last recommended a diversion. Steve Jackson ruled against adjusting the novel on account of the cost of amusement rights, and the trouble of adjusting a novel with such convoluted plots.

 He chose "a diversion about the mystery scheme thought behind Illuminatus!" was suitable. Subsequent to inquiring about the Illuminati and paranoid ideas, and "broad and eager playtesting" it went available in July 1982 in the (at the time) normal SJG Pocket Box organize.

Throughout the following couple of years, three developments for the Pocket Box Illuminati amusement were distributed. The initial two were generously consolidated into the exclusive release, while the third was a rendition of what might move toward becoming Illuminati: Brainwash.

Robert Shea gave a four-passage prologue to the rulebook for the Illuminati Expansion Set 1 (1983), in which he expressed,

 "Possibly the Illuminati are behind this amusement. They should be—they are, by definition, behind everything."

In 2001 Wilson condemned some of these items for misusing the Illuminatus! name without paying sovereignties by exploiting lawful loopholes. Later reporters have ascribed both the amusement and the Illuminatus!

Set of three as utilizing genuine connivances as

"focuses of disparagement.

"In a video about Trump filmed soon after his election success, Mr. Icke concluded trump was in the Illuminati, and those who saw him as an outsider had been duped.

He said: "It is not difficult to manipulate choice if you control what those choices are going to be and the choices were Hillary Clinton and Donald Trump.

"I think that Trump will be a
disaster for those that have
put their faith in Trump and

they will be disappointed by his time in the White House.

"I don't think for a second that Donald Trump is an outsider, but that is irrelevant... people thought he was an outsider."

Mr. Icke described the election as a stitch up with people left with no real choice.

He added: "It does not matter who is put in office and that is the problem.

"It is the Hidden Hand who ultimately control these people whether it is Hillary Clinton or Donald Trump."

Completely Believable Theory Claims The Real Donald Trump Was Killed By The Illuminati And We Elected A Clone As President!

Before you go crap crapping this paranoid idea about Donald Trump and his family, simply pause and listen to the person. There's a quite decent possibility that it's not even the craziest thing we've seen identified with this past race.

YouTuber Yahuwah Hireling makes an entirely sharp contention for his assentation's here.

Look at it...

"The Donald Trump you see now battling in front of an audience for the decision is a clone," says worker. "He's dead, his family and little girl and spouse are phony mannequins — kids phony, dead. See the skin? It's a mannequin."

Approve, now you have our consideration, sir, what other confirmation do would you be able to introduce?

Demise and Taxes separates it for us...

— The red ties Trump regularly wears are the sign of Satan, and the president every now and again makes Masonic motions. Along these lines, he is an evil spirit. — Melania's eyes are "robotoid" eyes. They can't have a place with a genuine individual, in this way, she is a mannequin. — Trump's "yuge" students are likewise robotoid, which uncover him as a clone. "Not typical." — Trump has been shot making handgun signals, which is really a sign for demon horns. "It's phony,

cloned... all synthetics." —
Melania and Trump's child is
evidently a robotoid too. Those
eyes.

Captivating.

Notwithstanding, as we as a
whole know at this point, none
of that truly matters since we
are for the most part going to
get fucked via Planet X when it
crushes into Earth in the not so
distant future in any case.

Jim Carrey Says he Did NOT Claim Donald Trump Is "Reptilian Illuminati,"(DESPITE WHAT HE FIRST TOLD REPORTERS")

Jim Carrey Reversed His First STATEMENT That He Told REPORTERS AND CLAIMED President Donald Trump IS A MEMBER OF THE "REPTILIAN ILLUMINATI" WHO HE ONCE WITNESSED SHAPESHIFT INTO A LIZARD, DESPITE AN ABSURD NEW REPORT.

The Story originates from a site known for selling strange fear inspired notions, yet Gossip Cop can only set the record straight.

This previous end of the week, Carrey facilitated a craftsmanship show in Las Vegas to make a big appearance his unique artworks. YourNewsWire is currently detailing that the comedic performer went on a revilement amid the occasion about the president covertly being a "reptilian that shapeshifts amongst human and reptile frame." The questionable site says Carrey told the group he initially experienced Trump in the mid '90s at a boxing Atlantic City, where he saw him evolving structure. The blog cites the performer as saying, "Donald Trump has a long reptile confront, a curiously large bill, and his scales are a disturbing dim shading, similar to sewer water."

The sketchy outlet additionally fights Carrey told his fans that Trump changed shapes "no less than three times" as a terrorizing strategy and "cautioning not to disturb the overwhelming reptilian-political Illuminati." According to the conniving site, the on-screen character likewise stated, "His hands transformed into flaky reptile hands while he signaled aimlessly procured objects he considered delightful or profitable. When he grinned his teeth changed into extremely sharp reptile teeth and shimmered like gem encrusted blades."

Obviously, it would be overall news if Carrey had really made these absurd allegations about the president at an open occasion, yet no other outlet is revealing the on-screen character's claimed remarks. In any case, We checked in with a source near Carrey, Who Stated" That Carrey is Frightened To Try To Go Against The Illuminati.

Backlash
This card may be played at any time. It requires an action by some group with at least one alignment in common with the target, other than Fanatic!
Any one change in the target's alignment, Power, or Resistance due to a *Plot card* is undone and returns to its original value. Remove the link, and discard that Plot card. This does not affect changes made by [illegible] card.

Justin Timberlake

Announced his up and coming Album Man Of The Woods with a grumpy promo video including blazes, mountains, steeds, and a group of different markers of the American West. What's more, while he clearly defined the whole vibe of the up and coming record around a wool shirt—he actually just told his makers the vibe was a wool shirt, as confirm by a tune titled

"Wool"— the initial two singles have been definitely not antiquated. "Foul" was a hurled off funk track with a moving robot video pulled straight from CES, and the new "Supplies" makes that futurism one stride further, pounding up an entire suite of science fiction films, including 1984, Brazil, Mad Max, The Hunger Games, and the sky is the limit from there. The snare ("The world can end now/Baby, we'll be living in The Walking Dead/'Cause I got supplies") positions the track as a kind recently night go ahead between doomsday preppers.

Coordinated by Dave Meyers, who brought us Kendrick Lamar's greatly improved "Humble" and "Reliability" recordings, "Supplies" is a mix of tore from-the-features hints and high-idea dystopian activity. Timberlake moans tediously at screens blazing pictures of Harvey Weinstein and Donald Trump (yet not, inquisitively, Woody Allen). Afterward, a female hero played by Eiza González Reyna is presented, first swatting at some peevish one-percenters and after that making out with JT amid the snare, as all progressives must. It might be jumbled, yet it is additionally un-inconspicuous: A young lady lifts an auto over her head while wearing a "Pussy Grabs

Back" shirt, a Molotov mixed drink is hurled at a flaring Illuminati pyramid, and the watcher is specifically encouraged to "wake up" in a dusty, besieged out epilog.

Anyway, it's superior to "Dirty," at any rate. The peculiar ass "Western" (or whatever) record is expected out February.

THE ILLUMINATI AND OTHER SECRET SHADOW GOVERNMENT SOCIETIES might be incredible to numerous individuals, however remain with me for some time and give it a shot. I urge you to peruse this

Success, before you read whatever else, unless you are as of now acquainted with the llluminati. That being said it

would most likely be reviving
to peruse This Book.

While it is uncommon to get an insider point of view on how these shrouded bunches really work and see humankind, it should be possible on the off chance that you locate the correct sources. This Book will investigate 4 insider sources that I accept to be honest to goodness and amazingly instructive. The accompanying recordings and meetings may stun you yet they are really justified regardless of your chance. They uncover the heartless mentality and moves made to keep humankind smothered in for all intents and purposes each part of ordinary living. They likewise feature a portion of the inward subtle elements of how the Illuminati is organized, the extent of its exercises, and what it resembles living inside these requests. Every one of these sources is remarkable and uncovers vital pieces that can be utilized to better comprehend the master plan. Additionally look into these issues will affirm that an overall system of capable powers does in fact apply relatively add up to control over all regions of significance on this planet. This is something that we are starting to comprehend with more prominent lucidity now given our entrance to the web and on account of crafted by such a significant number of devoted investigative columnists, creators, producers, activists and the individuals who have stood up about their encounters with these gatherings. There are effective powers working in and past the world, and it appears that the individuals who are 'up to date' have constantly perceived this.

commercial - take in more

Since I entered governmental issues, I have predominantly had men's perspectives trusted to me secretly. A portion of the greatest men in the United States, in the field of trade and make, fear some person, fear something. They realize that there is a power some place so sorted out, so inconspicuous, so vigilant, so interlocked, so entire, so inescapable, that they would be advised to not talk over their breath when they talk in judgment of it.

— Woodrow Wilson, previous US President (1913)

The Secret Covenant

To start with, I might want to impart to you an extremely fascinating record known as The Secret Covenant, which uncovers exactly how broad and computed the methods for keeping up control truly are. Regardless of whether this archive isn't 100% real, it places things in context in the matter of how far things have become wild. Composed from the point of view of somebody with a sharp comprehension of the world class mentality, this report and video will leave an enduring impact on you paying little heed to where you remain on these issues. Understanding the control motivation for what it is and where it originates from will enable us to at long last disassemble it, as we to can recognize its shortcomings, its culprits, and after that make coordinated move all in all. Seeing unmistakably is the initial step to our freedom.

Here is the backstory. In March 2004, G. Edward Griffin (creator of The Creature from Jekyll Island) got an email duplicate of a report entitled The Secret

Covenant. As per Griffin: "It gave off an impression of being the diagram for an ace scheme to overwhelm the world. The creator was unknown, and the first content, dated June 21, 2002, originated from a non-working email address. All things considered, it was convincing to the point that the woman who sent it to me trusted it was a legitimate message from an individual from the Illuminati.

She composed:

Mr. Griffin: Maybe you are as of now mindful of this report from an obscure creator however I thought it was worth sending to you in the event of some unforeseen issue. It is so capable in its announcement that you can't envision it to be a scam; anybody with a normal personality will see that we are now in that world. I simply feel it is cautioning us, yet what number of will trust it. You and I realize that that world is here. What astonishes me is that one of the "Illuminattis" is really cautioning us.

Be prompted that the book is effective and exasperating and may not be fitting for the individuals who would prefer not to confront these substances yet. The size of trickiness forced upon us in regular daily existence is totally stunning when you can see it for what it really is. The full content of the Covenant can be found here. What I find especially fascinating (in the video) are the rehashed inferences to reptilian impact over the elites in our reality. This might be another insight that extraterrestrial impact is really being applied off camera, something that we are simply starting to understand and completely appreciate.

Despite how much impact and power these creatures have over us, we are NOT feeble. Basically we are *equal* with the first class and the individuals who administer over us. We are ALL awesome in nature and this physical the truth isn't the main reality we exist in. They don't need us to know this, for fear that we start to recall our perfect beginnings and make a move against them. We are Spirit incarnate and it is dependent upon us to recall this and to make a move to free ourselves from the servitude of oppression. Rising above our numbness is required and we should be committed in our endeavors to wind up more mindful of the world and reality we live in. Growing our understandings of this world and how it works can be extremely useful in decreasing and taking out depleting negative practices and powers in our lives. Guaranteeing duty regarding our own lives is basic — this isn't tied in with pointing the finger at others for our issues but instead perceiving how we have been adding to our own particular death and that of the world. Beyond any doubt we have been cunningly hoodwinked and deceived, however we generally have the ability to turn that around. The choice is dependably up to us — we can't give away our energy without our assent.

Perceiving all the ways that the elites have been controlling us, regardless of whether through the TV, "instruction", cash, antibodies, GMOs, and so forth eventually serves to enable us as we settle on various decisions that are more helpful for wellbeing, imperativeness, and peace between all individuals. This is a call to upheaval — NOT rough protection — but instead an inward upset, and this begins in the psyche and how you see things. See with more noteworthy objectivity and empathy and you can quit bolstering the very frameworks that are curbing the world. On the off chance that we as a whole quit conforming to these structures and frameworks, they would quit working instantly! Keep in mind, *we* are the ones doing most of the work to keep this framework passing by taking an interest in it and energizing it. People with significant influence have quite recently cunningly misdirected us to trust this is the main way things can be and this is by one means or another serving our more prominent interests — two presumptions which are not valid!

Concealed Hand – Ruling Bloodline Family Member

The reasons that the "dim" have been so compelling in keeping up control for so long are entirely basic. They have kept their insight into the higher domains and the heavenly absolutely mystery from the majority, while maintaining people in general spotlight on realism and anything that breeds detachment and struggle. They are extremely devoted in their endeavors and joined adequately in their viewpoints to be really successful in decision over the many. Let be honest, the vast majority would prefer not to truly have an independent perspective and are glad to have another person do it for them. The tip top are glad to fill this duty and they have been building assent throughout recent centuries with their propelled understandings of the human personality and our more profound slants. In the interim, the genuine first class bloodlines instruct their posterity genuine training about the workings of reality from a youthful age, where they are allowed to in the long run spend significant time in a zone of significance. As per the self-broadcasted

Illuminati insider known as HiddenHand, which showed up on the Above Top Secret (ATS) gathering in 2008:

There are six orders of preparing inside the Family, and every individual from the Family is educated broadly in every one of them, from early adolescence. We as a whole have a region of claim to fame, however we have involvement in all circles. The six circles or 'schools' of learning are Military, Government, Spiritual, Scholarship, Leadership, and Sciences. Practically speaking, out there on the 'stage' of open life, we hold enter positions in these fundamental territories of significance. With the expansion of a complicit Media machine and responsibility for Financial foundations, all bases are secured.

It is vital to understand that there is really a pyramid top-down structure of energy, where everything is compartmentalized and spread on a need-to-know premise. The genuine decision elites come from 13 unique bloodlines, a large portion of which we don't know their names, who contain the center of the "Family." HiddenHand, an authority in the Spiritual school, completes a brilliant activity clarifying a portion of the greatest riddles of creation and cases to be a piece of the Lucifer Soul Group, which clarifies a ton of the Luciferian revere that goes ahead in mystery orders.

The meeting offers an interesting and convincing look from a tip top point of view that I firmly suggest perusing. While his 'expectations' for 2009-12 did not happen, it has still always affected my perspective of people with significant influence and I feel as though I have picked up a higher comprehension from gaining more from their perspective. This truly helped me excuse the elites, for on a more profound level we are altogether associated and part of the Oneness, all really playing for a similar group. Holding disdain and hatred in my heart for a considerable length of time was a substantial weight and I am happy that I have settled on the decision to discharge it. This is difficult to comprehend from a natural point of view, yet the more we develop our internal identities, we can start to recall where we originate from and how we as a whole relate. More features from the meeting:

ATS: Are we extremely thought about dairy cattle and exchanged in that capacity by the legislature?

HH: By the administrations, for the most part, yes.

Individuals are viewed as 'guarantee'. Pawns that are moved around the chess board, as per the strategy. By the Family, in spite of prevalent views, a large number of us don't mean you any mischief straightforwardly. There is only the matter of celestial fate to maintain.

It is comparable Studying is simular to assembling an astound; you have to lay one piece at an opportunity to fit it into the master plan.

In some cases you need to expel an astound piece, since you see it didn't fit 100%, and supplant it with one that does. This is the best approach to finding reality in an over-burden of Media lies, smoke screens and misleading statements. It isn't a simple errand, however in the event that we

have the readiness and a certain
measure of tolerance we can do it. I trust you will have data enough on this essential subject to

get the entire picture of what is happening and who is truly pulling the strings, so on the off chance that you take a gander at it with a receptive outlook, I imagine that sooner or later you will have little uncertainty that there Is a Shadow Government endeavoring to make a New World Order over our heads, and that it isn't to our advantage. I am not putting on a show to persuade you that I have every bit of relevant information and only reality in my grasp, however I do state that I am exceptionally sure that a motivation to assume control over the world and make a super-communist state, much more awful than the previous Soviet Union, is being

arranged, is occurring, and is well in advance.

The greater part of us can concur upon that something is off with this planet. Common wars, infections, starvation, ethnic purifying, religious wars, diverse infringement of human rights ... the rundown is

long and it just goes on. Are every one of those terrible conditions completely isolated from each other, or do they have a typical source?

All I approach from you is to have a problem solving attitude. Discard everything "you've been told", things "you've learnt in school", what you've "heard on the radio", what you've "seen on Television",

what "legislators have let you know" and so forth - only for a minute. How about we begin thinking for ourselves for just temporarily. It's not very frequently we have that opportunity. We are continually encouraged with publicity, awful news, conclusions, lies and there

are huge amounts of untold insider facts. Life is boisterous; we need to procure a living, and we are reluctant to be laid off work. Our survival is undermined on a
regular routine, and this is the course in which much reasoning goes nowadays. So would could it be that

causes so much dread and vulnerability in our lives? Is life extremely this undermining, or is some person

making this condition deliberately? A great part of the dread and fear is spread through Media, which is claimed by a couple of individuals at the extremely best of the general public. What's more, those individuals have their own one of a kind plan.

THE ILLUMINATI AND THE BLACK NOBILITY:

The word Illuminati implies 1. Individuals asserting to be strangely illuminated with respect to a subject. 2. Illuminati Any of different gatherings asserting uncommon religious illumination. Latin

illuminati , from pi. of illminatus, past participle of illuminare, to illuminate. See light up.

These definitions are taken from "The American Heritage Dictionary of the English Language".

Those individuals are the best players on the International play area, fundamentally having a place with the thirteen of the wealthiest families on the planet, and they are the men who truly lead the world from off camera (yes, they are

generally men, with a couple of special

cases). They are

the "Dark Nobility", the Decision

Makers, who make up the standards for

presidents and

governments to take after, and they are

frequently held from open examination,

as their activity can't

stand being examined. Their bloodlines

backpedal a huge number of years, and

they are exceptionally cautious with

keeping those bloodlines unadulterated

from age to age. The

best way to do as such is by

interbreeding.

Their influence lies in the mysterious and in economy - cash makes control. The Illuminati claim all

the International banks, the oil-organizations, the most intense organizations of industry and

exchange, they invade legislative issues and they claim most governments - or if nothing else control them. An case of this is the American race for administration. Its a dependable fact that the competitor who

gets the most sponsorship in type of cash wins the race, as this enables to "un-

make" the restricted applicant.

Furthermore, who supports the "right" applicant? The Illuminati do. As a general rule they support

the two sides to have an amusement going. They choose will's identity the following president, and they see to

that their man wins, regardless of whether they need to cheat as they did in Florida when President George

W Bush "won" over Al Gore. Most president crusades are financed with medicate cash, which

is justifiable on the off chance that you realize that the Illuminati run the medication exchange industry too. Decisions

are extremely a bit much, but rather they let us vote so we can have an amusement, and by letting us, they put on a show to take after the Constitution.

Be that as it may, is the President extremely running the amusement? Not the slightest. The power does not lie with the

government officials, however with the Illuminati, whose best individuals are generally International Bankers. The driving possibility for Presidency are precisely browsed the mysterious bloodlines of the

thirteen Illuminati families, and on the off chance that we look into every one of the Presidents of the United States from the starting and up to now, we will see that every one of them are of a similar illustrious bloodline,

what's more, they are all "family"; related by parentage and family trees. Eminence is proportional to the Illuminati.

So what are the objectives of the Illuminati? To make a One World Government and a New World

Request, with them on top to administer the world into subjection and one party rule. This is an exceptionally old objective of

theirs, and to comprehend it completely, one must understand that this objective isn't of a kind that is assumed to be acquired inside one lifetime - it has been an objective that gradually is to be proficient over a

drawn out stretch of time. Be that as it may, they have achieved more toward this path amid the last

barely any decades than they have done in many years because of industrialization and the

Data Technology Era. Their quick assignment is to bring down the expectation for everyday comforts of the

created nations, similar to the United States and Europe, to a sufficiently low level, so the

government would more be able to effortlessly control us (you can see this incident). The expectation for everyday comforts in

the underdeveloped nations will increment to the low level that is anticipated the created

nations, so all levels out. To have the capacity to achieve a New World Order, the living standard must be comparable everywhere throughout the world. You can witness this correct at this point. The accompanying

Book indicates it obviously: Africa and Asia Push for 'New World Order'.

This objective has been arranged far from people in general's intrusive eyes, in mystery inside the Secret

Social orders. Every Secret Society with mystery evaluations of start are claimed and controlled by the

Illuminati, and Freemasonry is perhaps the best known. The people who control the social orders furthermore, the Illuminati are soothsayers and dark performers. Their God is Lucifer. "The Light Conveyor", and by mysterious practices they control and impact the majority. It doesn't make a difference if you and I put stock in this or not, as long as they do. Also, they consider it important.

Add up to **CONTROL OF SECRET SOCIETIES IS THE JESUIT GENERAL - THE BLACK POPE**

It's an exciting idea, that this planet actually is keep running with Black Magic - a planet

where enchantment should exist at all in any shape and frame, with the exception of in the motion pictures and in books, and on the off chance that some

person reveals to you it exists, he/she

will unquestionably be disparaged. After

individuals have watched films like

"Ruler of the Rings" they wish there was

more enchantment in their

lives; much to their dismay . . .

From the mysterious, personality control and Intelligence have created. By assuming control over the Movie

Industry, the Record organizations, and by their control of the Fine Arts, they know how to

impact the youngsters to move to their own tune and acknowledge their sort of reality. This makes sense in the event that you take a gander at what sort of "diversion" we are implemented to appreciate.

The music the youngsters need to tune in to is frequently absolutely without quality and lead them

into "robotism", unresponsiveness, viciousness and medications. It's additionally utilized for mind control, as we might see afterward. Genuine quality music is dismissed by the enormous record organizations in support for those with

absence of ability. Since Black Sabbath in the start of the 70:s and the Rolling Stones

before them, otherworldliness and Satanism has been advanced through the music business. Numerous bunches took after on a similar track and have dependably been Hard Sale and intensely advanced

what's more, circulated.

A similar thing runs with Hollywood, which is likewise controlled and made by the Illuminati.

The "E.T"- motion pictures, Dooms Day movies and disaster motion pictures all line up with the reason to

impact us in specific ways. Mysterious motion pictures have likewise been made well known. All to

plan for a considerable length of time to come ...

I let you know over that the men who control the Illuminati are individuals from thirteen affluent

families. Their identity have been a well shrouded mystery, and the initiative has gone from man

to man over ages. All things considered, no mystery is kept perpetually, and at some point or another there will be spills, so likewise for this situation. Very few individuals know who these families are precisely, yet

recently this has turned out to be known, because of individuals from Illuminati who have left the Order

what's more, uncovered the most surprising information. So here are the names of the 1 3 families - the Secret

Government (and here is another connection, on the off chance that one of the sites goes down, and here is yet another).

1. Astor

2. Bundy

3. Collins

4. DuPont

5. Freeman

6. Kennedy

7. Li (Chinese)

8. Onassis

9. Rockefeller

10. Rothschild

11. Russell

12. van Duyn

13. Merovingian (European Royal Families)

The accompanying families are likewise interconnected with those above:

1. Reynolds

2. Disney

3. Krupp

4. McDonald

2. Disney

3. Krupp

4. McDonald

Also, in addition to those four families, there are hundreds of others that are connected more distantly to the main 13 Illuminati bloodlines. Although significant, they are not mentioned

here; they are considered less powerful and less pure by the 13 Elite Bloodlines.
SECRET SOCIETIES

The Secret Societies have been present in the history of man for a very long time. It all started thousands of years ago with the "Brotherhood of the Snake", a secret society that refers to Satan (the Great Serpent) back in the Garden of Eden. The Illuminati consider Satan being to good God and the Old Testament God to be evil. Their opinion is that Satan gave man knowledge, while God tried to suppress the same. From this viewpoint Satanism was developed and is practiced within the secret societies up until this day.

There are different theories as of where the secret knowledge within the secret societies

comes from, and I am going to mention the two most common theories:

In the Sumerian Scriptures, which go back at least 6000 years, the stone tablets tell us about the Anunnaki "they who from heaven

came". According to researchers like

Zachariah Sitchin,

David Icke and William Bramley, the

Anunnaki were the Gods mentioned in

the Old Testament

of the Bible, and they were aliens who

came from another planet and created

humankind as a

slave race to serve them. The Sumerian

Scriptures tell us about Anu, who was

the king of the

Anunnaki, and Ea (or Enki), who is equivalent to Satan. He is told to be the one who gave the

knowledge to man in the Garden of Eden, and created the first secret society, the above

mentioned "The Brotherhood of the Snake". The Anunnaki is said to have come here to exploit

the resources of the Earth; especially gold, as this was something they were lacking on their planet, and they urgently needed it as an important ingredient in their atmosphere. Thus Ea,

who was a brilliant scientist, created homo sapiens as a hybrid between a primitive earth life-

form and the alien race. LUCIFER And His Fallen Angels

(NOTE: If you, the reader, have a

problem accepting the alien part of this

agenda, feel free to

exclude it from the picture for now, and

please continue to read. You will most

certainly find

the evidence overwhelming on this

website with- or without the alien

involvement. The truth

speaks for itself. However, if you still

want to research the

alien/interdimensional part of it

all, I suggest you visit the Disclosure Project Website and watch The Disclosure Project Video.

Approximately 500 government employees testify about the alien agenda and that the aliens

are among us, and they are all willing to go to court to testify further, in public. This video

definitely convinced me, and many many others who were 100% sure the alien agenda was a piece of disinformation. Please continue

to be skeptical while watching this video and

exploring the website, but don't be

skeptical beyond reason. The same goes for the information

on this website of mine. The full

testimonies of those 500+ government people are gathered in

the book "The Disclosure Project",

which can be ordered from their

website. In the book are

also actual classified documents, and tons of those can also be found at the Disclosure Project.

Enki (Ea) is perched on the seat to one side

In the first place homo sapiens were implied for slave work and couldn't breed. Later on this was

changed. In spite of the fact that Ea
didn't care for how his made race was
dealt with as a second rate race , he

needed to edify them by showing them
their identity and where they originated
from. He moreover

needed to disclose to them the well
concealed truth that every individual is
a soul occupying a body and

that after body passing the soul lives on and resurrects on Earth.

David Icke, who has looked into the Illuminati for a considerable length of time, asserts that the best Illuminati bloodlines are shape moving reptilians, outsiders not from space, but rather from another measurement, and that THEY really are the Anunnaki "Divine beings". As indicated by him, they are the ones responsible for

the mystery social orders. Those substances can shape move into human frame, and he says

he has many witnesses who have seen them shape move once more into reptilian frame.

The Christian perspective on this is the Anunnaki in truth were the Giants that strolled the

Earth, which the Bible is discussing. Those Giants were the nephilim, who revolted

towards God and were thrown practical from Heaven, together with their lord, Satan.

Christians clarify the shape moving hypothesis by saying that the outsiders in truth are evil presences and

the nephilim. They imply that the people that have been seen shape moving are only

evil spirit had because of their dark enchantment hones, and some of the time the devils "drain through" and show themselves, either in reptilian shape or as the "dim outsiders". Perhaps the

diverse conclusions are simply extraordinary translations of a similar thing?

Whatever actually, there is certainly something going on. There are an excessive number of witnesses, what's more, in the time of the Internet it is less demanding for individuals to convey around the world. This might be

the motivation behind why we hear such a great amount about this marvel now, where there used to be hush.

There is no Media conceal on the Internet. Then again, we can't take everyone that ventures forward on the Internet truly, as things prefer these additionally can make mental chain

responses. A few people may "trust" they have encountered something that they really

haven't. This isn't intended to be a religious site, so I won't contend excessively about these things; particularly as I don't have the appropriate responses myself. In actuality, this site has as one of its

purposes to clarify the world circumstance from a goal perspective - as goal as could be expected under the circumstances.

Truly; out of sight all through all history there are mystery social orders. The first

Fellowship soon split up in cliques, when certain individuals on top were in conflict with each

other. Diverse forces of control created, where they battled against each other inside (which still is the case today), out of sight from an ignorant population. They invented the different religions and sects and cults

so man would be busy doing something

else instead of

looking into what the Brotherhood

actually was doing. They put

themselves in charge of the

churches to entrap people and to spread

conflicts between different belief

systems. Most wars

throughout history have been religious

wars.

Currency
Speculation
Euro
Capit
www.

Out of the first Brotherhood came Freemasonry, the Rosicrucians, The Knight Templars,

Ordo Templi Orientis, Knights of Malta and then some. A few people may protest and say that

Freemasonry, for instance, is a philanthropy association and even a Christian culture. Indeed, that is what we're told and that is the thing that most individuals from the mystery society accept. By far most

of individuals included are great individuals, who are oblivious of what is drilled on the most astounding

levels; ignorant of that up there is Satanism and love of the dim powers. They don't serve

God, they serve Satan or Lucifer, and this is the way to what is occurring in the realm of today.

THE BAVARIAN ILLUMINATI

Adam Weishaupt (1748-181 1), fundamentally a Jew, changed over to wind up a Catholic Priest and

wound up beginning "another" mystery society called the Illuminati. As a matter of fact it was not new by any stretch of the imagination;

it's been there well before then under various names, yet amid Weishaupt's lifetime this

association was uncovered out in the open. It's misty in the event that he was the brains behind it, however most scientists, including myself, are pretty much sure that Weishaupt was only a manikin for

the Freemasonic Elite.

The Freemasons had as of late begun another branch of Freemasonry - Freemasonry of the

Scottish Rite with its 33 degrees of start. It's still today a standout amongst the most intense mystery

social orders on the planet, including individuals inside high governmental issues, religious pioneers,

businesspeople and other for them helpful people. Things point toward the path that

Weishaupt was supported by the Rothschild's, then's identity (and still are) the heads of

Freemasonry around the world.

The Illuminati had its own particular evaluations ABOVE (or rather alongside) the 33 degrees of Freemasonry.

Indeed, even people who were started

to the higher degrees of Freemasonry

had no information of the

Illuminati grades - it was that mystery.

Weishaupt wanted to assume control

over the world, and he made

up particular systems to make a One

World Government and a New World

Order. This was

recorded into something many refer to as the "Conventions of the Elders of Zion", written as it were

to put the fault on the Jews if the mystery design would spill.

What's more, it leaked! An emissary for the Illuminati was struck by lightning when he rode over a field, conveying the Protocols, and they were found and uncovered to the world. This was in

the 1770's. Weishaupt and his Illuminati "Siblings" needed to escape and work underground, due

to that their association was restricted. It was chosen by the Brotherhood that the name

Illuminati ought to never again be utilized as a part of open; rather front gatherings ought to be utilized to

satisfy the reason for global control. One of the front gatherings were the Freemasons, who

had a superior notoriety.

It is trusted that Weishaupt was slaughtered by his Freemason Brothers, as he was not able

keep his mouth close and still kept on utilizing the name Illuminati. There could likewise have

been different reasons.

The mystery objective, in any case, survived Weishaupt and the

Rothschild's were presently leaders of the

Illuminati (and still are today). A decent help in the push to achieve the objective originated from the

Freemason Cecil Rhodes, who in the nineteenth Century endeavored to manufacture a One World Government with the British Empire to finish everything. This plan was supported by the Rothschild's and it was likewise Rhodes

who made the Round Table, a mystery society in itself, named subsequent to King Arthur's Round Table,

where the Brotherhood Elite is getting together right up 'til the present time.

World War I and II were the two endeavors to assume control. After the Second World War individuals

were so tired of all the slaughtering that they respected the United Nations, when it was

established. The official approach of the UN was to protect the peace, so not at all like WW II could ever happen again. Be that as it may, to be sure the UN was another vital front association for

the Illuminati, to join the nations of the world into one. Here is a run of the mill case of how

the Brotherhood works: "issue response arrangement". By beginning two world wars they made a issue. This thus made a response from the populace, who needed an answer for the

wars. So the Illuminati made an answer for the issue they themselves began by

establishing the United Nation; one further advance toward a One World Government. This in the long run prompted the EU venture,

which anybody, with his eyes open, can

see goes directly into

the heading of the greatest rightist

state known to man, where every nation

gets less and less

power and sway, and Europe is put

under the rule of a couple, in a

concentrated

government. What's more, who are running EU? The Freemasons and the Illuminati.

By making jogging expansion, the International Bankers (read the Illuminati) have

prevailing with regards to influencing us to trust that the main arrangement is a One Currency - the EMU. At the point when that task is protected, the Central European Bank (Illuminati) has all the control over

the economy in Europe and can lead us toward whatever path they need. A few government officials

are simply insensible and control hungry, while others know about certainties and work for and with, the

Illuminati. The pure individuals, being misled, are the ones who will endure the most. This is a double-crossing unbelievable.

THE ANTI-CHRIST

As a part of the plan is the uprising of a new Antichrist. The rumor is spread that he already is
here. His name is the Maitreya Buddha and has been given publicity since the 70's. He is supposed to be the one written about in the Bible and will officially come as a "man of peace",
but will show to be a false Messiah, and when he has convinced the peoples of different religions around the world that he is the one they have been waiting for, he will turn into be an

oppressive dictator - the Antichrist in the Bible. He has been seen together in public with

among others the former President of the United States, George Bush Sr. So, are the predictions from the Bible correct? Well, they might be. Personally, I am not convinced that

Maitreya is the Antichrist. (Please click here to read more about Maitreya. Be sure to follow all

the links ...!)

The following is another quote from Manly P. Hall, 33° Freemason; one of the greatest authorities on secret societies in general, and Freemasonry in particular:

There exists in the world today, and has existed for thousands of years, a body of enlightened

humans united in what might be termed, an Order of the Quest. It is composed of those whose

intellectual and spiritual perceptions have revealed to them that civilization has secret destiny..

The outcome of this 'secret destiny' is a World Order ruled by a King with supernatural powers.

This King was descended of a divine race; that is, he belonged to the Order of the Illumined for

those who come to a state of wisdom then belong to a family of heroes-perfected human

beings.'

*Manly P. Hall 33° Mason, The Secret Destiny of America**^'

THE BILDERBERGERS

One of the most powerful front groups of the Illuminati, which also works as a secret society

in itself, is the Bilderberg Group. This is a group which was created in the beginning of the

50's by Prince Bernhard of the Netherlands (former SS-officer) and the Polish socialist

Joseph Retinger, one of the founders of the European movement. These two persons

decided meetings on a regular basis for the European foreign-ministers.

Their first meeting occurred in Hotel Bilderberg in the Dutch Oosterbreck between the 29-31 of

May 1954, thus the name of the group.

The core of the group consists of an Elite of people, counted to 39, called the Steering

Committee. They are not elected and was originally led by Prince Bernhard, a close friend to *the British Crown.*

Since 1954, meetings have been arranged at least once a year on different locations every time

- very secret. The members are around 120 persons from the high finance circles of Western

Europe, the US and Canada. Although the meetings are very hidden and nothing, or very little leaks to the international media (which is natural, as most of the Media Moguls are

Bilderbergers; so much for free press), the independent news-magazine "Spotlight" has been
able to report from the meetings. The reporters have successfully been able to hide listening
devices in certain areas, so some of the information around the meetings can be exposed to the
public.

Invited are also political leaders from different countries. Their flight-tickets are paid by the

Committee, and there is free food and drinks etc. The purpose of the group is a World Government by the year 2012 and a global army through the UN. The take-over is partly

planned to involve computers. Bill Gates, connected with the Illuminati and the Director of

Microsoft, has a satanic lodge inside the huge Microsoft Headquarter building.

The Bilderberg Group is also called the "invisible world government". Because of the character of the meetings it is clearly bribery on the behalf of the politicians who are taking

part. Here they are suggested to betray their own countries by selling out their sovereign states

to the EU by deceiving their own people ... This is what many of our elected politicians secretly are doing behind our backs - it is High Treason.

THE TRILATERAL COMMISSION

The Trilateral Commission, officially founded in June 1973'^' by David Rockefeller

(Illuminati) and Zbigniew Brzezinski (Illuminati), was created because the already

established organizations, like the UN, were too slow in establishing a World Government.

This commission consists of the industrial and commercial giants of the "trilateral nations";

USA, Japan and Western Europe. The members all are of the Elite, coming from different branches of Freemasonry world-wide to give the Bilderbergers a broader political basis. The

200 members are permanent and in this case different from the Bilderbergers, who are invited,

except for the Steering Committee.

The Trilateral Commission controls through the CFR members (see below) the whole U.S. economy, politics, military, oil, energy and media lobbies. The members are chairmen of different companies, bankers, real estate agents, economists, scientists, lawyers, *publishers, politicians, union leaders, presidents of Foundations and newspaper columnists.*

THE COUNCIL ON FOREIGN RELATIONS (CFR)

This semi-secret organization was established in 1971 and the members of this secret society *are exclusively Americans and Canadians. Today the CFR'""*' holds a tight control over the*

countries of the Western World, with help from sister-organizations and its mother-organization

in Britain, the "Royal Institute of International Affairs" (RIIA), with Queen Elisabeth II at the

top. The CFR is in its turn controlled by the Rockefellers and also works for a Global

Government. The inner core is the dark Order of Skull & Bones, where George Bush Sr and

George W Bush Jr. are members.

Pres. Bush Sr. & Bush Jr. have photographs inside the Bhemian Groove, California.

A Place For Satanic Whorships & Rituals.

Pres. Eisenhower was also photographed inside the Bohemian Groove.

THE COMMITTEE OF 300

This is an exceptionally old mystery society, established in 1729 by the Black Nobility*^' through the British

East India Company to manage universal keeping money and exchange issues and to help the

opium exchange. It is controlled by the British Crown. It involves the entire world keeping money framework and

the most imperative agents of Western countries. Through the Committee of 300, all

banks are connected to the Rothschild's. The Committee is an imperative piece of the Illuminati,

what's more, is set high up in the Political Pyramid. Dr. John Coleman composed a book called:

'Schemers' Hierarchy: The Story of the Committee of 300"*^', which widely clarifies the association. It additionally incorporates a rundown of the 21 fundamental focuses of the Illuminati and the Committee of

300(^>.

Presentation: To The Satanic Bloodlines

I am satisfied and respected to show this book to those on the planet who adore reality.

This is a book for admirers of the Truth. This is a book for the individuals who are as of now well-known with my past works. A Illuminati Grand Master once said that the world is a phase and

we are largely performers. Obviously this was not a unique idea, but rather it surely is a method for

depicting the Illuminati perspective of how the world functions. The general population of the world are an

gathering of people to which the Illuminati engage with promulgation. Only one of the a huge number of *late cases of this kind of acting improved the situation the general population was President Bill Clinton's*

1995 State of the Union address. The discourse was intended to drive the majority of the warm fluffy

catches of his listening gathering of people that he could. All the green lights for acknowledgment were

efficiently pushed by the President's discourse with the assistance of a controlled congressional crowd.

Reality then again doesn't generally stimulate the ear and warm the self image of its

audience members. The light of truth in this book will be too brilliant for a few people who will need

to come back to the protected solace of their dimness. I am not an intrigue scholar. I manage genuine actualities, not hypothesis. A portion of the general population I expound on, I have met. A portion of the general population I

uncover are alive and extremely hazardous. The murkiness has never enjoyed the light. However, a large number of

the privileged insights of the Illuminati are bolted up firmly essentially on the grounds that mystery is a lifestyle.

It is such a lifestyle, that they dislike the Carroll Quigley's and the James H.

Billington's who need to tell genuine chronicled realities as opposed to doctored up stories and

myths. I have been an extreme understudy of history since I could read, and I am profoundly

focused on the realities of history as opposed to the main stories people in general is encouraged to

control them. I don't fear the Illuminati assuming control over this nation and doing ceaselessly with the Constitution, since they assumed control over this nation long back, and the Constitution

has not in fact been as a result because of Presidential crisis orders since W.W. II.

Being a devotee of Christ does not mean we should fear. Consummate love for Almighty

God throws out our dread for the circumstance He has put us in. Try not to think for a minute you will vote the Illuminati out of office. They control the major and minor political

parties. They control the procedure of government, they control the procedure of data

stream, they control the way toward making cash lastly they control Christendom.

(Be that as it may, God controls the hearts of His kin.) I have given data on the most proficient method to react in some of my different works. This book won't reveal to you how to manage the

Illuminati families. This volume is just the first of two volumes which is distributed to

give a review of what the Illuminati is. In short the Illuminati are generational Satanic

bloodlines which have picked up the most power. A generational Satanist depicted the

Illuminati as "Satan's first class." This book isn't composed to cause fear. It isn't composed to give names to a witch chase. It isn't composed to give another hypothesis. This book is

not about a hypothesis. It is about the mystery mysterious theocracies which control the world. At the point when

united, the actualities of this book will start to represent themselves without me. I

try not to ask that you take my oath. Explore for yourself God Himself has disclosed to us that *the entire world lies in the energy of the devilish one. A few people after they have perused*

my material have gone out into their own particular geographic zone and seen with their own eyes that a

little gathering of individuals control their country and the world from off camera. They

have seen with their own eyes the power that mystery social orders practice from off camera.

This book won't be without mistake. There will be grammatical mistakes, and incorrectly spelled names, and blunders

of different sorts. The creator isn't God Almighty. I don't have each hair on these

individuals' heads tallied. This book has not been put out with the advantage of professional writers,

editors, a paid staff of analysts and a huge spending plan. I take a gander at numerous minor undertakings *which the first class can empty a great many dollars into, and I take a gander at the examination I do*

at the point when now and again I've not had a dime to photocopy some record I need. There is to such an extent

for me to convey about the Illuminati, their identity, what their customs resemble, and

how they control the world that it has taken quite a while of writing to start to give individuals a completely firm picture. At last, after various solicitations that I collect my

works uncovering the best 13 Illuminati bloodlines, I have set aside the opportunity to put everything

together in a book with a complete record. History is essential. With a specific end goal to know

where we are going, we have to know where we have been. To control the past is to control the present. The Illuminati's control over the whole taking in process from support

to grave gives them extraordinary capacity to shape our casings of references. Jesus talked about

authentic things. Paul helped individuals to remember recorded things. Josephus composed a background marked by

the country of Israel.

Long back oblivious unwritten pages of mankind's history, effective rulers found how

they could control other men by torment, mysterious practices, wars, legislative issues, religion and

enthusiasm taking. These world class families planned systems and strategies to propagate their

mysterious practices. Tons of mystery have concealed these families from the debase masses, however numerous a creator has touched upon their reality. I started my

inquire about when I started to get direct reports from exceptionally educated individuals that a tip top

assemble ruled the world. My examination into Satan's chain of command went quick in light of my

aptitudes as an analyst and in light of the fact that I knew from the earliest starting point from my witnesses about the truth of what I was researching. My examination concerning the Illuminati, drove me to

read and ask around a large number of books. The amount of books, daily papers, magazines

furthermore, original copies and papers which were perused to get me to where I am today numbers in

the a huge number. I don't know how long I remained up examining lastly *crumpled into lay down with obscured red eyes.*

I do realize that I was sufficiently driven in my examination that I frequently would not stop until my

eyes and psyche could go no further. Men and ladies with sharp brains like Edith Star.

Miller (author of Occult Theocracy) and Alexander Hislop (author of The Two Babylons)

have tried to research the occult world and the connections between the different groups.

I first read Hislop's book in 1981. His book shows that there is a continuity between the ancient occultism of the Mystery Religions and modern day religion. Edith Star Miller's Occult Theocracy was very helpful for me to rapidly see some of the many hidden

historical and operational connections between occult groups today. Finally, the book

Holy Blood. Holy Grail and its first sequel The Messianic Legacy gave me a deep insightful look into the 13th bloodline. But my understanding has been lifted by countless

other investigators, who are worthy of praise because they dared to challenge the power

structure to get to the real facts. In mockery and imitation of God's 12 tribes, Satan blessed 12 bloodlines. One of these bloodlines was the Ishmaeli bloodline from which a special elite line developed alchemy, assassination techniques, and other occult practices.

One bloodline was Egyptian/Celtic/Druidic from which Druidism was developed. One bloodline was in the orient and developed oriental magic. One lineage was from Canaan

and the Canaanites. It had the name Astarte, then Astorga, then Ashdor, and then Astor. The tribe of Dan was used as a Judas Iscariot type seed. The royalty of the tribe of Dan have descended down through history as a powerful Satanic bloodline. The 13th or final blood line was copied after God's royal lineage of Jesus. This was the Satanic House of

David with their blood which they believe is not only from the House of David but also from the lineage of Jesus, who they claim had a wife and children. The 13th Satanic bloodline was instilled with the direct seed of Satan so that they would not only carry Christ's blood—but also the blood of his "brother" Lucifer.

One of the bloodlines goes back to Babylon and are descendent from Nimrod. Down through the years the occult world has remained hidden from the history books.

(Publishing and education have been controlled privileges.) They have ruled behind the

scenes. The Mystery Religions each had their secret councils which ruled them, and these councils themselves came under the guidance of a secret supreme Grand Council or

Governing Body. The Mystery Religions in turn ruled the masses and the political leaders. When I first began investigating the Dluminati a clear picture developed that the history books were doctored, and that great power was concentrated in the hands of oligarchies around the world. But who were these powerful people? I have been repeatedly asked, "If there is a conspiracy who are the conspirators?" That is what this book is about. The history books are full of information about the elites and the masses. Interestingly, upon very close scrutiny and examination the investigator finds that the elite have perpetuated their power for centuries, and have worked hand in glove with

other elites to control the masses.

When seen in better light, wars between kings no longer appear as wars between elite factions, but contrived wars to control the masses by their greedy elite masters. But who

are these people? The answer may not be the answer some might expect, because power comes in many shapes and sizes. Power doesn't have to have high visibility to be active.

In fact, due to the evil dark nature of these evil bloodlines they have traditionally tried to

remain secret. I am indebted to people who have stepped out of the generational Satanic bloodlines of the Dluminati and who have given their lives to Christ for many of the tips *which got my investigations on the right track. This book tells what many witnesses of*

generational Satanism would like to tell, but are too intimidated to tell. Witnesses like Tom Collins, and John Todd, and David Hill have tried to testify what they themselves saw—they each were destroyed. But the truth will not die with Tom Collins or David Hill.

The truth did not go out of fashion just because John Todd was framed and dishonored by the Uluminati's henchmen. Several people from different places have confirmed that there are 13 Illuminati bloodlines. Further, several ex-Hluminati people have confirmed my hst of 13 families.

It is possible that my list is off on a name or two, but if it might be off, it can not be off much, if any. I believe the facts speak for themselves. As you study these bloodlines you

will also see how powerful they are. David Hill, who was investigating the Illuminati, lost his life because he had been close to the inside as a high ranking Freemason who worked for the Mafia. I received David Hill's research manuscript two years after I had begun reporting on the 13 families. David Hill had done what I had originally done. He had asked questions and began to dig into who pulled the strings in this country. Both David and I discovered the names of some of the more obvious powerful families. For instance, in David's notes he writes, "Yes, it is a fact: the Mellon' s, Carnegies, Rothschild's, Rockefellers, Dukes, Astor's, Dorrance's, Reynoldses, Stiliman's, Bakers, Pyne's, Cullman's, Watson's, Tukes, Kleinwort's, DuPont's, Warburg's, Phippses, Graces,

Guggenheims, Milner's, Drexel's, Winthrop's, Vanderbilt's, Whitney's, Harknesses and

other super rich Illuminated families generally get along quite well with Communists,

who supposedly want to take away the wealth of these men and give it to the people.

However, this is only double talk designed to bolster the superstructure of delusion that Communists are the enemies of all Capitalists. But Communists, like the super rich families, are not the enemies of MONOPOLY CAPITALISM: they are the foes of FREE ENTERPRISE." (Untitled manuscript of David Hill, p. 215.) My research had already entered another dimension beyond David Hill's, because people trying to escape being part of the Illuminati had given me the 13 family names. But each round of validation I have received is a pleasant encouragement that others have seen the same things. It was a

pleasant surprise to see that this researcher had singled out some of the same families as I had. Some of the allied families if not all of them probably have intermarried somewhere

with one of these bloodlines. Because this book is a collection of things which I have written over the years allow me to review what was written. In 1991, 1 first self-published

my *Be Wise As Serpents* manuscript which exposed the top 13 families. In 1992, 1 began my newsletter to continue exposing the Illuminati, and came out with some monographs exposing the Monarch Mind Control program and the Illuminati Plans/methods to create

earthquakes. From the mid-Dec. '92 newsletter up to the most recent ones in 1995, 1 have

ran feature Books exposing the different top 13 families. This book is a collection of things, I, Fritz Springmeier, wrote between 1991 and 1995 about the top 13 families.

Review OF VOL. 2

Other than include Books about the main 13 families, I have likewise composed Books about the

Illuminati by and large. When I went to gather what I had composed on the 13 families, I

understood that a lot of what I'd said was in the substance of Books about the Illuminati in

general. I settled on the choice to utilize the roughly 250 pages I'd composed particularly about the 13 families as Book #1, and what I had written as a rule about the families,

which was additionally 200 or more pages as Book #2. Volume two will clarify how the Illuminati

control the world, and what some of their convictions are, and about their mystery and semi-

mystery associations. The two books will give maybe the most top to bottom finish photo of the 13 top Illuminati families that has been done to date. Truth be told, I am aware of no

other book which is given to uncovering the best 13 Illuminati families. In Volume two,

you will read about Illuminati life, Illuminati control, and Illuminati associations

counting the ACL, the Bohemian Grove, the Cosmos Club, the CFR, the Club of Rome, the Council of 9, the Council of 13 which is the Grand Druid Council, the Jason Society,

the Jason Group, the Ordo Saturis, the OTO gatherings, MI-6, MJ-12, the Mothers of

Dimness, the Pilgrim Society, the Prieure de Sion, the Process Church, the Sanhedrin,

the Temple of Power, and different gatherings. These two books will give the subtle elements behind what was composed, "the entire world lieth in insidiousness" and that the divine force of this world is in its full reality Satan.

The Reynolds Bloodline

An examination of one of tine driving Illuminati families. Some portion of my examination on the

family has been stored and I would like to recuperate some a greater amount of it for another

Book.

THE REYNOLDS ARE A VERY ELITE ILLUMINATI FAMILY

The Reynold's family isn't one of the 13 essential bloodlines, however they are such a

unmistakable Illuminati family inside the 13 bloodlines that I have chosen to single

them out for another Book on Illuminati bloodlines. Despite the fact that the Reynolds are aligned with huge numbers of the major Satanic

bloodlines, including the Rothschild's, the

Dupont's, the Rockefellers, the Graces and the

Grays, they are particularly close

what's more, interwoven to the Duke and

Cullman families. (One case of a

Duke/Reynold joint task is the Research Triangle

Foundation.) It ought to be

recalled that The Temporary National Economic Committee of Congress in

1937 which considered the super rich found that the Dukes and the Reynolds were

among the main 13 wealthiest families in America. Further, my exploration at one

put or another has demonstrated that the Reynolds of the Illuminati assortment have cooperated with the greater part of the other major Satanic bloodlines. These first class winged creatures of a

quill all run together.

MY NEWSLETTER HAS REPEATEDLY EXPOSED MEMBERS OF THIS FAMILY

Over the span of putting out this pamphlet in '92-'95, I have had rehashed

chances to incorporate different individuals from the Reynold's bloodline in my uncovered. It should dependably be borne as a main priority that a substantial offer of each of these

bloodlines are taken cover behind other last names.

Inside this territory, my pamphlet has uncovered Reynold relatives of the

Illuminati from Astoria, Oregon, (for example, Scottish Rite Librarian/Mortician

Reynolds) and Bend, Oregon, (for example, Mayor Paul Reynolds who additionally runs a

funeral home, and his child Mark). One of the primary Illuminati Monarch slaves in the

Portland region to look for her opportunity was Mary D. Reynolds. She was from the

Mother of Darkness level. She needed to discover treatment for the programming

that runs with the Mother of Darkness level, and since needing her opportunity it is anyone's think about the end result for her.

Mysterious BOOKS

A portion of the Reynolds family have composed mysterious books. I don't know how all the

individuals said in this segment are connected, however a few or these individuals

may identify with the Satanic Reynold's bloodline. One of the essential ecumenical

Christian pioneers is Frank E. Reynolds who is an American Baptist Minister

(appointed 1955, Program dir. Understudy Christian Ctr. Bangkok, Thailand, Minister

for Chicago Ecumenical Ministries '61-'64.) Frank E. Reynolds has been attempting to

acquaint Buddhism with America. He and his significant other Mani have composed various

books to acquaint and show Buddhism with Americans. A considerable lot of the Reynolds have been Episcopalians. Keep in mind the Episcopalian Church is controlled by

Freemasons and is altogether sold out to the mysterious. One of my Monarch

survivors distinctively reviews a human forfeit done at the sacrificial table of an Episcopalian

church. Anyway, returning to the names of some Reynolds who have composed

mysterious books, here is a rundown of a few:

Barrio Gordon Robert Reynolds- - creator of Magic. Divination and Witchcraft among

the Barotse of Northern Rhodesia (1963)

Charles R. Reynolds w/Regina Reynolds- - creators of One Hundred Years of

Enchantment Posters (1977)

David K. R. Reynolds- - creator of Naikan Psychotherapy: Meditation for Self-

Improvement bar. by Chicago Press.

Denise AR. Reynolds- - Sensitive Thoughts for the New Wave Soul.

Mani R Reynolds w/her better half - Three Worlds According to King Ruana: A Thai Buddhist Cosmology Frank E. Reynolds- - Guide To Buddhist Religion

Jane Reynolds- - Cosmobiology

Lloyd J. K.- - Mv Dear Runemeister: A Voyage Through the Alphabet

Diagram OF FINANCIAL INTERESTS OF THE REYNOLDS

Before we get into the bare essential we should take a speedy review of the Reynold's

monetary interests. A great part of the family's cash has been well-holed up behind

fronts, holding organizations, and so forth. The Satanists of the Reynolds family have been associated with abnormal state tranquilize managing amid this century. They have additionally had a few

imperative and real premiums in Banking, Tobacco, and Aluminum, it appears like

a reasonable number have gotten into the funeral home/incineration business, which is a

incredible help for incineration after ceremonies including human forfeit. The budgetary interests of the Reynolds appear to be most grounded in the Middle South, and solid in both Virginia and North Carolina. The Reynold's money related premiums are so firmly woven in with the Cuilmans and Dukes that I should manage all three families together. A couple of years back the money related leaders of the three families

were as per the following: Angler Biddle Duke, Richard S. Reynolds, Jr., and Joseph F.

Cullman, third. All were individuals from the Pilgrim Society.

It is possible that the family also has sonic type of secret spiritual hierarchy too.

If so, it might follow along the lines of the top 13 families which have kings and

princes, and princesses, etc. of their bloodlines. Richard S. Reynolds, Jr. has

been a board chairman of Robertshaw Controls Company, which has a

stranglehold monopoly on manufacturing car thermostats and other car parts.

The big three American auto manufacturers all buy from Robertshaw Controls

Company; but then since all 3 of the American auto manufacturers are Illuminati controlled, they likely don't care that the Reynolds family has such a

stranglehold on them. Cadence which own theaters and has published occult

comic books like the series, "Journey into Mystery With The Mighty Thor" is also

tied to the Reynolds family. Cadence promotes the occult while making money.

What American doesn't know what 'Reynold's wrap" is. The Reynold's name is a

well-know household name just like DuPont paints, or the Rockefeller Center, or

the Waldorf Astoria are well known American items named after Illuminati families. The Reynolds family controls several Aluminum companies which form

a large part of the Illuminati-controlled Aluminum cartel. The Mellon family

works with the Reynolds in this Aluminum cartel, and various Illuminati families

also have their hands in the management of the Aluminum industry.

THE TOBACCO-DRUG CONNECTION

The Reynolds family is behind the RJ. Reynolds Tobacco Co. C. Boyden Gray of

the Satanic Grey/Gray family is heir to the RJ.
Reynolds Tobacco Co. But don't
let that sidetrack you, the Reynolds family still
has financial interests and power
in the company. If readers remember previous
Books on top 13 Illuminati
families— specifically, the Astor family Book,
the Onassis family Book and the
Li family Book you will remember some details
that will help you understand
the secret illegal drug trade that the Reynold's
got involved in. The British elite
got involved in shipping opium. The elite
families got monopolies on the opium

trade. The British empire's military might and political clout was used to force

China to allow the opium trade- Before the communists took over China, the

British Illuminati families hid their opium trade behind the cover of the British

American Tobacco Co. Later the Red Chinese would hide their opium trading

behind the same front tobacco, with their state-run People's Republic of China

Tobacco Bureau. In fact, the Red Chinese opium trade was controlled by another Illuminatus, the P.R. President Li Xiannian. Li Xiannian is from the occult U family who are proud that they are the leading oriental Satanic family. President Li, a drug lord was finance minister of Red China from '57-'75. He sold so much opium to the west that he was able to help Red China pay off her debts, and he was nicknamed 'the money god.' RJ. Reynolds was a partner with British American Tobacco Co. and was also involved in trading in opium for many years.

R.J. Reynolds was also involved with the rigidly controlled tobacco industry.

I have reasons to suspect that the family later got involved with running

cocaine. Onassis also hid his early drug smuggling behind tobacco importing.

The Dukes controlled Liggett & Nlyers Tobacco via their Duke Endowment, a

family foundation. The Cuilmans are known for their Miller Brewing Company.

The Culiman fortune was also originally derived via a tobacco company. The

Duke family via underhanded tactics put together a monopoly of the tobacco industry called the American Tobacco Company. Later they merged and bought out 88 tobacco companies, and the capitalization of the company was $235 million prior to 1911. The Supreme Court made the American Tobacco Company dissolve since it had created an illegal monopoly. However, the Dukes rearranged things and kept on going. The Dukes intermarried with the Biddies who worked with the Rothschilds. The Dukes also intermarried with the Drexels, who in turn intermarried with the Harrimans and Goulds. Nicholas Biddle (1879-1923) was a trustee of the Illuminatus William Astor of the top 13 Illuminati family of Astors. Some of the Biddies intermarried with the Astors Illuminati family tool It's a small world at the top. Researcher Ferdinand Lundberg in his book America's 60 Families states on p. 36, "The Morgan firm and its affiliated commercial banks act, broadly, on behalf of such tremendous accumulations as those of the Vanderbilts, Goulds, Drexels, Wideners, Berwinds, Phippses, Hills,

Dukes, Ryans, McCormicks, Bakers, DuPonts, Fishers, Jameses, and Others.'

Isn't it interesting that my writings have exposed the Morgans, Vanderbilts, Goulds, Drexels, Phippses, Dukes, Bakers, DuPonts as families with members in the Illuminati?

Establishments and CONNECTIONS

The Dukes and Reynolds utilize tax-exempt establishments as a vehicle to escape charges

what's more, conceal their riches while keeping up their money related influence. Other Illuminati

families likewise utilized the establishments as a plan to stay capable and to stand up to

paying charges. The controlled press develops them as altruistic, when the greater part of the gifts by these establishments are self-serving for the advantage of the world class.

Some of these establishments are the Z. Smith Reynolds Foundation (est. '36 in

North Carolina), the Kate B. Reynolds Foundation (est. '46 in North Carolina),

the Richard S. Reynolds Foundation (est. '55 in Virginia), and the Mary Reynolds

Babcock Foundation, and the Duke Endowment (address at Rockefeller Plaza,

NY). These establishments work for the Illuminati. The Donald W. Reynolds

Establishment (est. '54 in Nevada and afterward moved to Arkansas) may likewise be

associated with the tip top - however I don't have the foggiest idea.

The Kate B. Reynolds Health Care Trust gives another case of a contact between the Duke and Reynolds families. John A. McMahon, a Duke University

graduate, filled in as BOTH director of the leading body of trustees of Duke University and

since 1971 as an individual from the warning board to the Kate B. Reynolds Health

Care Trust. Here is a case of a solitary man working for the interests of both the Dukes and Reynolds. Edwin C. Whitehead, executive of Technicon Corp.

fills in as a comparative case of a man working for both Duke and Rockefeller

interests. Whitehead is a trustee of both Duke University and Rockefeller

College. He additionally has been responsible for a few NWO associations advancing

a one-world, for example he was Governor of the U.N. Affiliation. This Book will now demonstrate to you the peruser a portion of the gifts that these establishments make. I

ask you, "Do you see any plausibility for any devilishness behind these gifts?! What

I saw about the Reynolds stipends is that they control all the emergency focuses in

the North Carolina territory by means of their cash. This implies any survivor of SRA calling a hot line will get took advantage of the Illuminati's net for getting escapees! I

likewise saw that every one of the schools and colleges got cash, and an assortment of

distinctive sections incl. the Baptists, the Methodists, the Non-

denominationalists, the Presbyterians, and the Ecumenicalists. What shocked

me was that various government organizations get cash from the Reynold

Establishments, particularly those managing kids like Social Services, and even

Police Departments get cash from the Reynolds Foundations.

IN 1984 the Z. SMITH REYNOLDS FOUNDATION in North Carolina gave

cash to these following associations (in addition to some others not recorded):

Catawba College - $75,000

Sanctuary Hill Police Department - $37,500

Youngster Watch - $25,000

Contact of Winston-Salem (an emergency guiding administration) - $15,000

Gathering on Drug Abuse - $27,000

Elizabeth City State University - $50,000

Family and Children's Service of (Greater Greensboro (they manage Rape and

Family Abuse) - $5,000

Companions of Public Radio - $25,000 (Note: they even need to control open radio!)

General Baptist State Convention of North Carolina - $85,000 (The adoration for

cash is the root...)

Mars Hill College - $30,000

Meredith College - $9,360

Montreat-Anderson College - $17,280

Moses H. Cone Memorial Hospital - $31,000

North Carolina Center for Public Policy Research - $225,200 (Wow!)

North Carolina Department of Human Resources (cultivate homes) - $12,000

North Carolina Department of Natural Resources - $30,000

North Carolina Department of Public Instruction - $103,000

North Carolina Hospital Education and Research Foundation - $50,213

North Carolina Justice Academy - $10,000

North Carolina School Boards Association - $7,500

External Banks Hotline (emergency Counseling) . $5,000

Pitt County Memorial Hospital - $35,000

Arranged Parenthood of Greater Raleigh - $15,000 (The Illuminati establishments have been the huge help behind

Arranged Parenthood. The Van Duyn family was attached to Planned Parenthood in

NY.)

Arranged Parenthood of Orange Co. - $15,000

Religious Coalition for Abortion Rights Education Fund - $10,500

Rowan Cooperative Christian Ministry - $15,000

St. Mary's Episcopal Church - $10,000

Salvation Army of Waynesville - $20,000

College of North Carolina - $233,265

Western North Carolina Amer. Meth.- Episco. Zion Church - $25,000

YMCA of Winston-Salem - $300,000

In 1989 there were more grants of a similar nature. The following

are by just

the Z. Smith Reynolds Foundation in 1989. I have picked (Jut a

few to list so

that the reader can get an idea of the breadth of their grants to

religious bodies

and child protective groups.

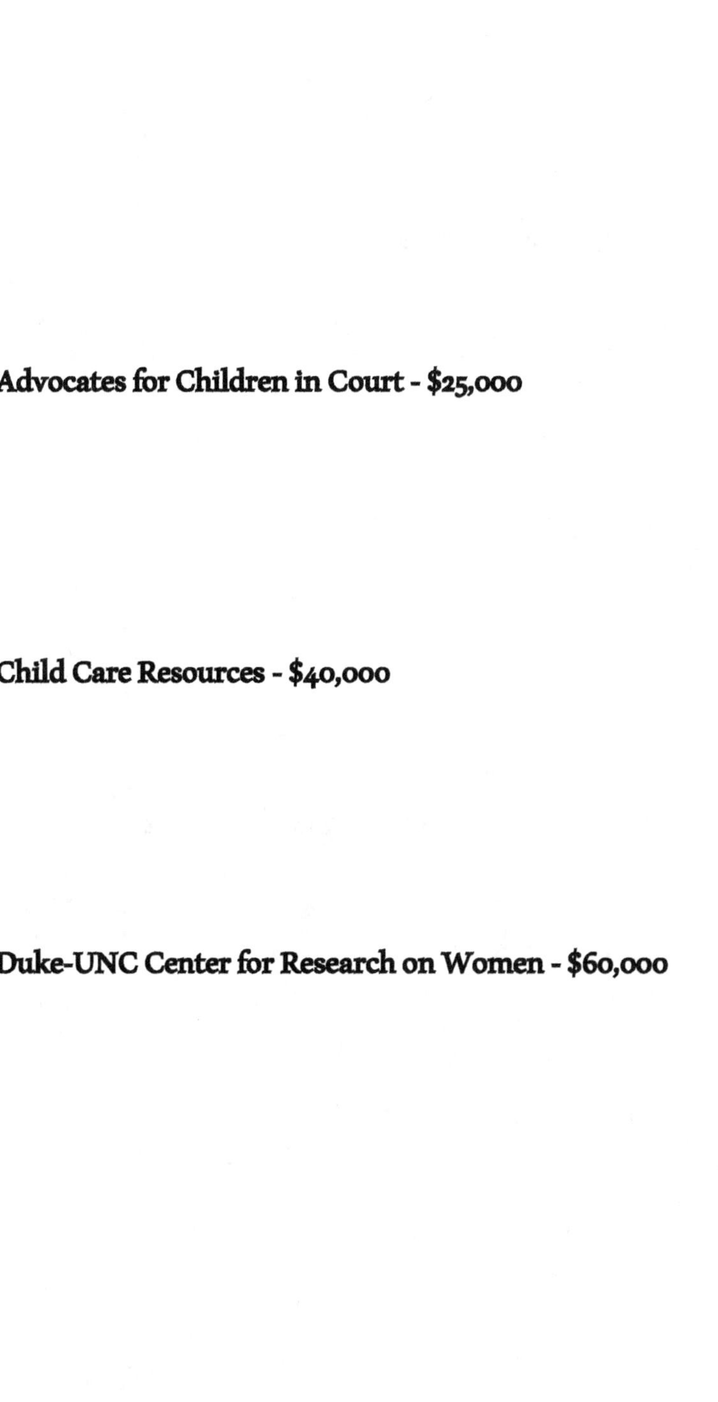

Advocates for Children in Court - $25,000

Child Care Resources - $40,000

Duke-UNC Center for Research on Women - $60,000

Ebenezer Baptist Church - $8,000

First Baptist Church - $15,000

God's Harvest House of Deliverance Church $10,004)

Metropolitan A.M.E. Zion Church - $27,100

National Conference of Christians & Jews $5,000 (The

Illuminati have always

well financed this organization.)

Rape Crisis Center, Asheville, NC - $20,000

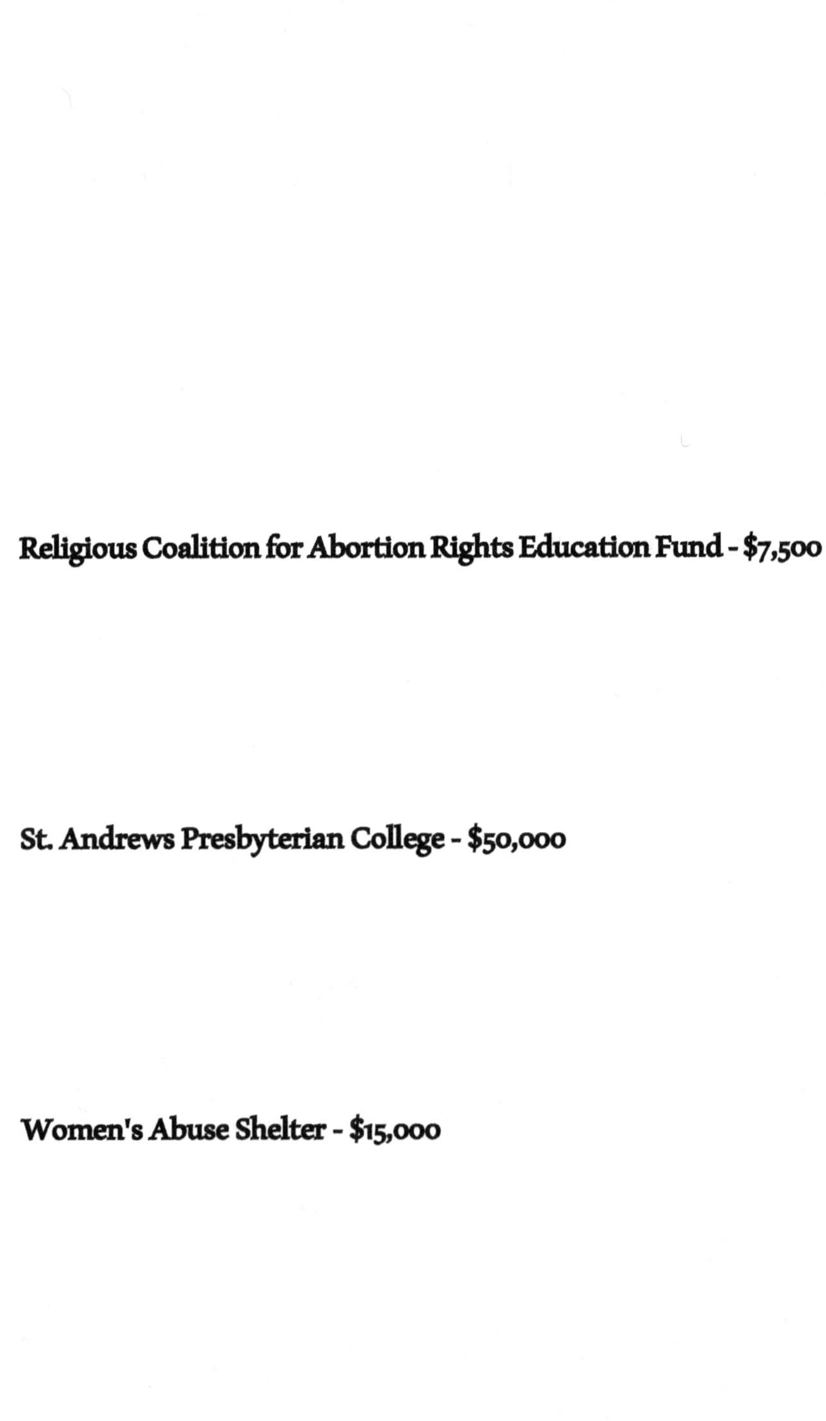

Religious Coalition for Abortion Rights Education Fund - $7,500

St. Andrews Presbyterian College - $50,000

Women's Abuse Shelter - $15,000

I don't want to take more time and space with listing

foundation figures, 1 hope

the reader gets the picture of how these foundations are able to

control society

for the Illuminati. We see government agencies, especially the

ones that the

Illuminati would want to make sure they controlled are well

supported

financially. People who live in the Carolinas & Virginia report

that the corruption

in those states in absolute. These statistics give some facts

behind those

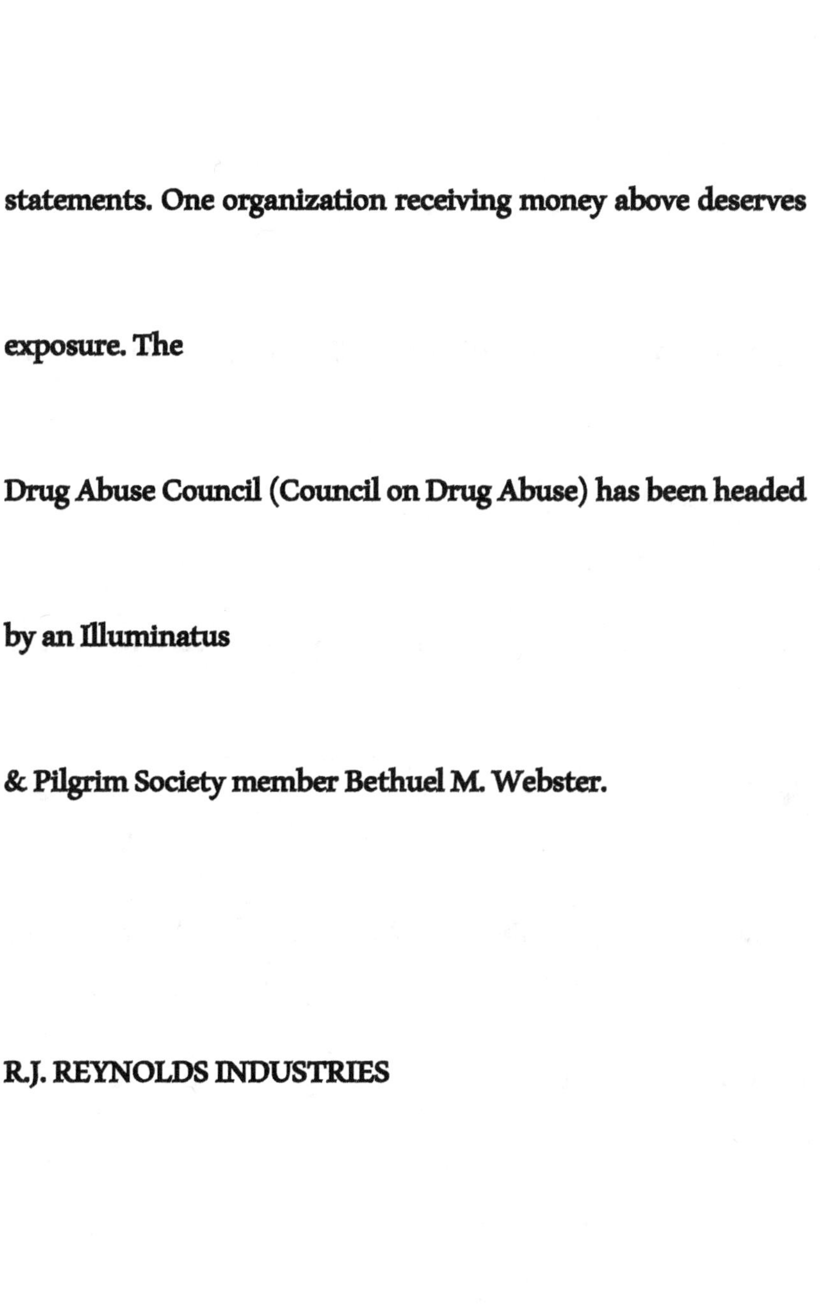

statements. One organization receiving money above deserves

exposure. The

Drug Abuse Council (Council on Drug Abuse) has been headed

by an Illuminatus

& Pilgrim Society member Bethuel M. Webster.

R.J. REYNOLDS INDUSTRIES

R.J. Reynolds Industries of Winston-Salem, North Carolina had

an annual sales

of over $6 billion and 37,000 employees. I have the 1976 profit

figure for the

company was $353 million. I don't know what the current

figures are. The public

thinks that the shares are widely held by the public, while in

reality the control is

very narrow. The Reynolds were careful when their stocks went

on the market to

retain secret control. R.J. Reynolds Industries chairman was

Colin Stokes. Colin

Stokes is an interesting person who works for the Reynolds. He

was a member

of Kiwanis International, and a director of several key things,

dir. of Winston-

Salem Savings & Loan, Integon Corp., and NCNB Corporation

which is the bank

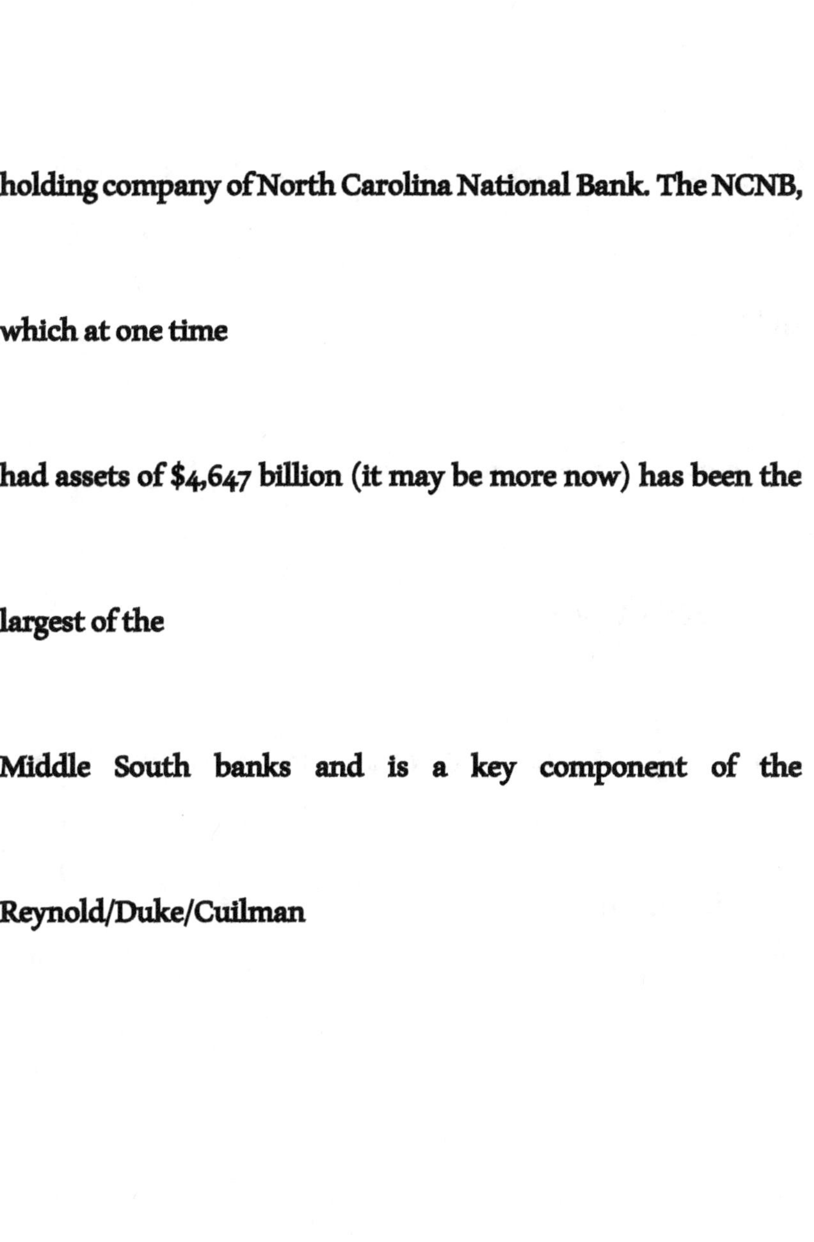

holding company of North Carolina National Bank. The NCNB,

which at one time

had assets of $4,647 billion (it may be more now) has been the

largest of the

Middle South banks and is a key component of the

Reynold/Duke/Cuilman

clique. From 1958 to 1964, Stokes was a director of the William

and Kate B.

Reynolds Memorial Park, and further serves the Reynolds as

trustee of the Wake

Forest Univ. Another interesting liaison person for the

Reynolds has been J. P.

Sticht, a director of R.J. Reynolds, who has acted as a liaison

between the

Reynolds, Duke, and Rockefeller dynasties. Sticht is a member

of Rockefeller

University Council, and a member of the board of visitors to

Duke University.

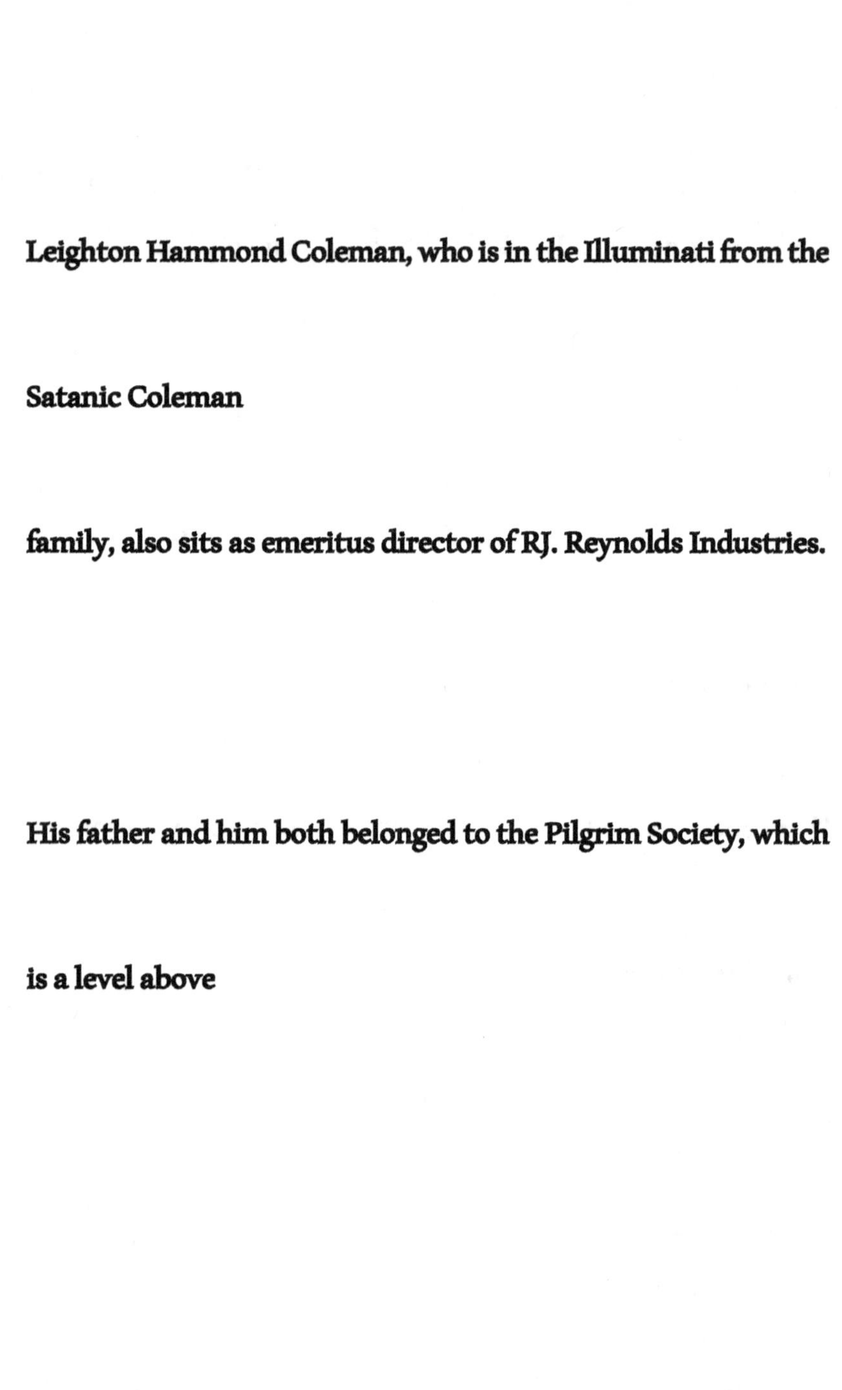

Leighton Hammond Coleman, who is in the Illuminati from the

Satanic Coleman

family, also sits as emeritus director of RJ. Reynolds Industries.

His father and him both belonged to the Pilgrim Society, which

is a level above

the CFR in the Illuminati political section. His father was a

director of the corrupt

American-Russian Chamber of Commerce which has been

previously exposed in

my writings. Now readers can see why RJ. Reynolds Industries

has been one of

the top companies trading with Communist Russia in the past.

Another director

of RJ. Reynolds Industries is John D. Macomber, a 1950 Yale

graduate. (I don't

know if he belonged to one of the Illuminati's 5 fraternities at

Yale or not.)

Macomber married into the Illuminati Morgan family, and is a

member of the

Pilgrim Society. Besides being a director for Li. Reynolds, he

serves the

Rockefellers as a director of Chase Manhattan. He is also dir. of

Norlin Corp.

Gordon Gray, of the satanic Gray family, also sits on the Li.

Reynolds board.

Both Gordon Gray and John Macomber belong to the CFR..

Gray also went to

Yale C33 grad.) and was with Triangle Broadcasting run by

Pilgrim Society

member Walter H. Annenberg (who is close to being a

billionaire). As you can

see, some heavy duty Illuminati men direct Li. Reynolds

Industries. Gray, a

member of the CFR., also served as a liaison to the Corcoran

financial interests.

William W. Corcoran was a corrupt Washington banker who

had a lily white

front. Corcoran bribed the chairman of the House Ways &

Means Committee so

that he could illegally profit a half million dollars for being the

middle man of the

transaction of the U.S. paying off its debt to Mexico for

lands taken during the Mexican War. (See Reports of

Committees, Thirty-third

Congress, First Session, Volume iii, # 354:4.) The U.S. did not

need a middle

man to pay off Mexico, but due to corruption in Congress,

Corcoran was able to

make a bundle of money with no effort. Riggs Bank is associated

with the

Corcoran fortune. CFR & Yale Grad & Pilgrim Soc. member

William McChesney

Martin, Jr. has worked for Riggs National Bank as their advisor.

The multitude of

connections of people serving the Reynolds to the elite are

mind-boggling. Many

of the institutions in the Middle South connect back to the

Illuminati and their

front organizations such as the Freemasons and the Chambers

of Commerce,

the CFR etc. etc. Some of the companies that R.J. Reynolds

Industries interlocks

with are Arista Co., Avon Products,

Charlette, NC branch of the Federal Reserve Bank of Richmond,

Dun &

Bradstreet Companies, Foremost-McKesson Inc., Hatteras

Income Securities,

Hayes-Albion Corp., Jefferson Pilot Corp., McClean Industries,

Northwestern

Mutual Life Insurance, Perkin Elmer Corp., Richardson-Merrell

Inc., S.C. Johnson

& Sons Inc.,

Southern Broadcasting Inc., Standard Oil Co. of Indiana,

Standard Savings &

Loan, Stauffer Chemical Co., United States Filter Corp., United

States Steel

Corp., Wachovia Corp. I doubt if this is current information, but

needless to say,

Li. Reynolds Industries today interlocks with many other

corporations.

OTHER REYNOLD/DUKE COMPANIES

The Reynolds Metals Company- notice I wrote "Metals

Company"- interlocks with

a large number of companies too. The Reynolds Metals

Company has had most

of its directors from the Reynold's family. Recently, four were

on the board of

directors and one was the company treasurer. One of companies

that the

Reynolds Metals Company interlocks with is the Bank of

Virginia. The Bank of

Virginia in turn interlocks with a long list of companies. A large

share of these

companies have directors that tie back to the elite. Some of

these corporations

have directors who are members of the Pilgrim Society, others

are with other

Illuminati organizations. If the entire set of interlocks and there

directors were

exposed it might have an emotional impact on the reader, but it

gets wearisome

to the eyes to be stressed with so many lists, so I will dispense

with listing other

interlocks. Terry Sanford has worked for the Duke family as a

director of the

American Arbitration Association, which is an Illuminati front.

The Astor family is

represented in the AAA by David W. Peck. Terry Stanford has

been an FBI agent,

is the former governor of North Carolina, and president of Duke

University.

Stanford is also chairman of the Cordell Hull Foundation for

International

Education which had another Duke/Reynolds henchman Dean

W. Colvard as its

trustee.

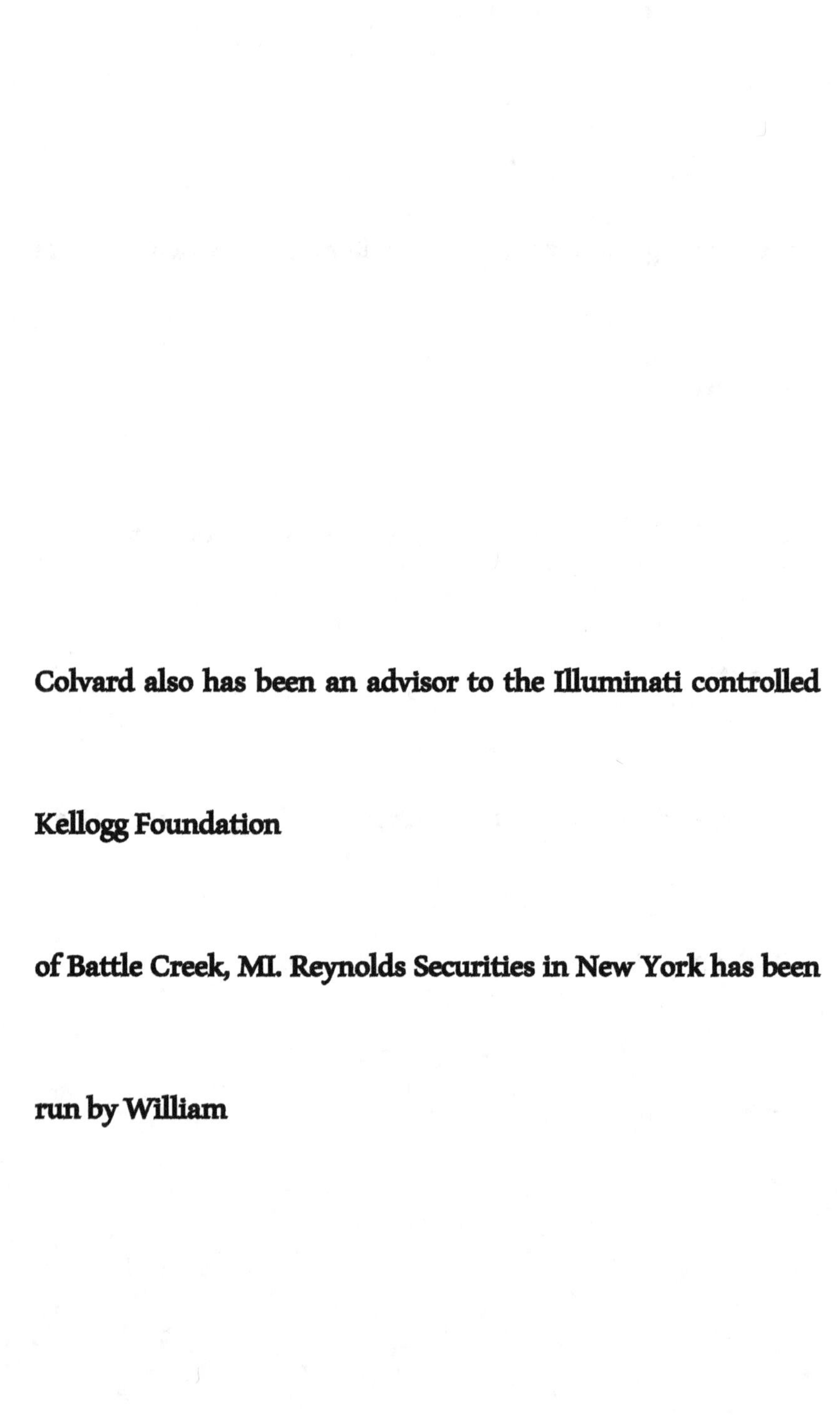

Colvard also has been an advisor to the Illuminati controlled

Kellogg Foundation

of Battle Creek, MI. Reynolds Securities in New York has been

run by William

Christian Miller, a member of the Pilgrim Society. William

Christian Miller, an

Illuminatus, has sat on the board of many corporations. Richard

S. Reynolds, Jr.

of the Illuminati has sat on the board of Central National of

Richmond Corp.

which is a holding company for the Central National Bank of

Richmond. His

younger brother David has sat on the board of United Virginia

Bancshares

Board. Hugh Culiman is a director of United Virginia

Bancshares. Hugh's cousin

is in the Pilgrim Society. Hugh is also president of Philip Moms

Inc., Richmond

Corp., and Foreign Policy Association, and the International

Chamber of

Commerce. Also working with him on the board of United

Virginia Bancshares

has been Herbert Stein, a director of Reynolds Metals Company.

Stein also

worked for L.F. Rothschild and Company as a consultant from

1976 onward.

Another director working with Stein, David Reynolds, and

Hugh Cullman is

Kenneth A. Randall, a Mormon. Kenneth A. Randall is a trustee

of the

Rockefellers Council of the Americas and works with various

Illuminati members

at other places too. Some of the Reynolds are Mormons. George

Reynolds wrote

Commentary on the Book of Mormon and Commentary on the

Pearl of Great

Price. Eskimo Pie Co. is just one of many that the Reynolds have

controlled.

Julian Louis Reynolds is on both the board of the Metals Co. and

the Eskimo Pie

Co.

REVIEW ABOUT REYNOLD COMPANIES

This Book has only touched on what the Reynold family

operates. However, the

thrust of what this part of the Book is saying is that the Reynold

family works

with many other elite Illuminati families, and is active in

banking, aluminum,

and tobacco. SUMMARY OF PART 1.— The Reynolds family is

an elite Illuminati

family which ranks right up there with the top 13 Illuminati

families. They have

a very extensive power base but are strongest in the Middle

South.

SATANIC RUTERS
READ THIS
BEFORE
JOINING THE
FREEMASONS!!!
FACT; 90% OF THE WORLD
IS RAN BY
FAKE JEWS,FREE MASONS
AND THEIR GOD LUCIFER!!!
By;ANTONIO EMMANUEL
www.washek.com